JUNIOR JEWISH COOK BOOK

by Aunt Fanny

Designed by EZEKIEL SCHLOSS
Drawings by CYLA LONDON

KTAV PUBLISHING HOUSE, NEW YORK

Copyright, 1956
BY KTAV PUBLISHING HOUSE

Dear Junior Cook:

This Junior Jewish Cook Book is written especially for you. The recipes are simple, and each step is outlined clearly, so that you will easily be able to follow all the directions.

The recipes are for foods you like to eat, and we hope you enjoy making the recipes as well as eating them.

Notice too, that the Cook Book is divided into holiday sections. Every section contains a short story of the holiday and its customs and ceremonies, and every recipe has been placed in its very own holiday section.

You will learn to make different kinds of holiday delicacies, so you'll be able to prepare menus for your very own parties!

You'll have a wonderful surprise for Mother too, because you are going to keep your kitchen neat and clean, Mother will never guess that you've been working there.

We hope you have lots of fun cooking!

Aunt Fanny

All the recipes in this book are in accordance with the Jewish dietary laws.

CONTENTS

EQUIPMENT	6-7-8
EQUIVALENTS	9
BEFORE COOKING RULES	10
AFTER COOKING RULES	10
MEASURING SUGGESTIONS	11
SAFETY RULES	11
COOKING TERMS	12
RULES OF ETIQUETTE	13
HOW TO SET YOUR TABLE	14

SABBATH — 15
- Candlestick Salad — 16
- Sabbath Delights — 17
- Fried Fish — 18
- Boiled Noodles — 19
- Candied Sweet Potatoes — 20
- Potato Kugel — 21

ROSH HASHANAH — 22

YOM KIPPUR — 22
- Honey Carrot Tzimmes — 23
- Rosh Hashanah Clusters — 24
- Stuffed Eggs — 25
- Honey Cookies — 26
- Baked Potato — 27

SUKKOS — 28

SIMCHAS TORAH — 28
- Flag Salad — 29
- Penuche — 30
- Carrot Raisin Salad — 31
- Baked Bananas — 32
- Meat Burgers — 33

CHANUKAH — 34

- Chanukah Cookies — 35
- Chanukah Latkes — 36
- Marshmallow Pops — 37
- Draydel Salad — 38
- Pancakes — 39

CHAMISHAH OSOR B'SHEVAT — 40

- Stuffed Dates — 41
- Stuffed Prunes — 42

PURIM — 43

- Prune Filling — 44
- Hamantaschen — 44
- Party Lemonade — 45
- Purim Hat Cookies — 46
- Queen Esther Salad — 47
- Noah's Ark Cookies — 48

PASSOVER — 49

- Seder Plate — 50
- Charoses — 51
- Passover Kugel — 53
- Passover Macaroon — 54
- Peanut Brittle — 55
- Candied Apple Wedges — 56

LAG B'OMER — 57

- Hints for Sandwich Making — 58
- Lag B'Omer Bulls Eye — 59
- Chocolate Peppermints — 60

SHEVUOTH — 61

- Cracker Cheese Blintzes — 62
- Tomato Flower Salad — 63
- Quick Truffles — 64

EQUIPMENT

ICE TRAY   CASSEROLE

STRAINER   WOODEN FORK

DOUBLE BOILER   WOODEN SPOON

APPLE CORER   WOODEN BOWL

GRATER   PARING KNIFE

PANCAKE TURNER   COLANDER

GRIDDLE   SAUCEPANS

MUFFIN PAN	CLOCK
SPATULA	SCISSORS
COOKIE SHEET	POTS
EGG BEATER	POT HOLDERS
MEASURING CUPS	PAPER TOWEL
LONG FORK	BUTTER KNIFE
COOLING RACK	BAKING PAN

TONGS	SHALLOW PAN
LONG SPOON	TABLE FORK
FRUIT JUICER	MIXING BOWLS
MEASURING SPOONS	VEGETABLE BRUSH
FLOUR SIFTER	CHOPPING KNIFE
KITCHEN TABLESPOON	BREAD BOARD
FRYING PAN	SLICING KNIFE

EQUIVALENTS

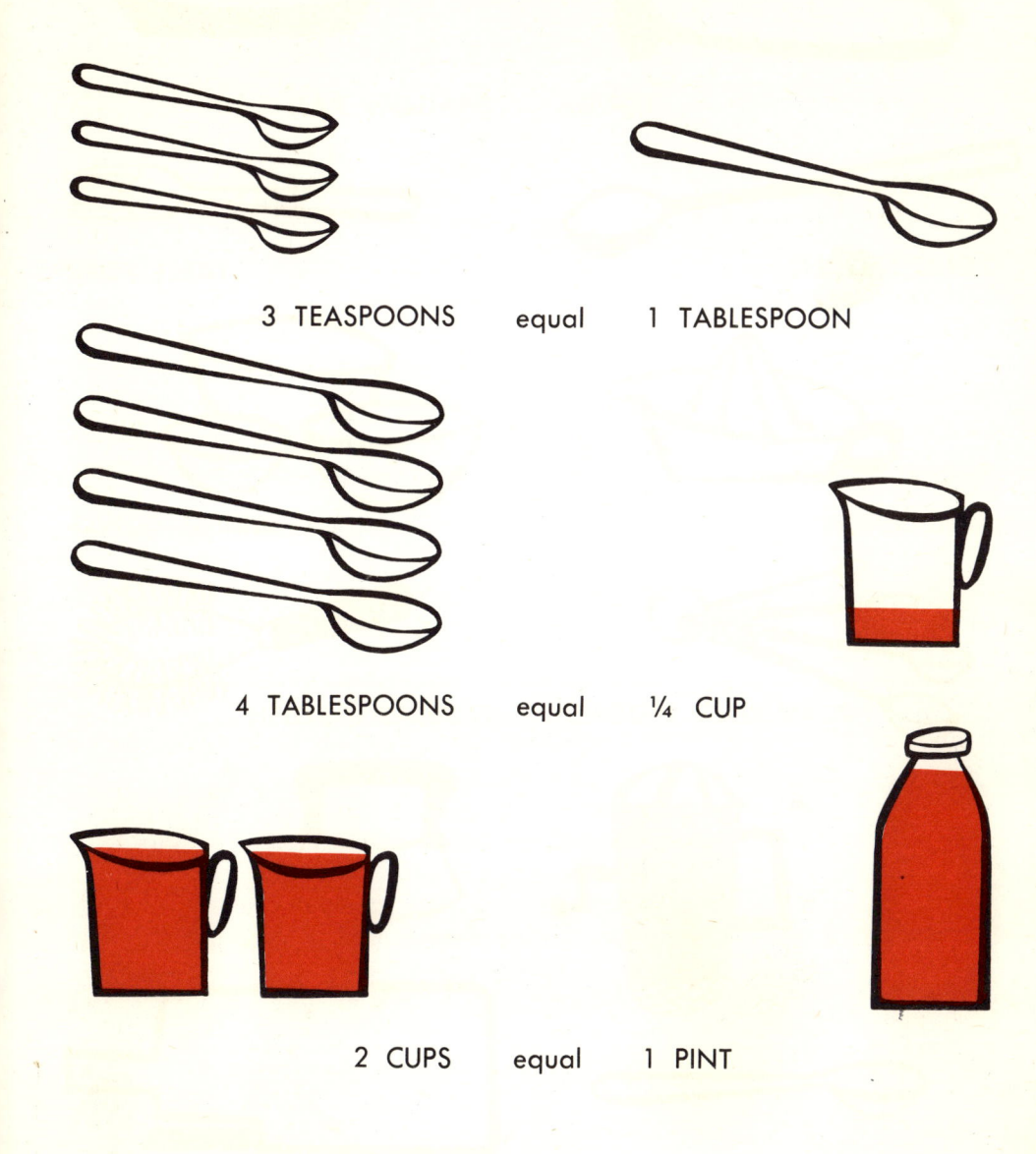

3 TEASPOONS equal 1 TABLESPOON

4 TABLESPOONS equal ¼ CUP

2 CUPS equal 1 PINT

¼ POUND BUTTER equals ½ CUP

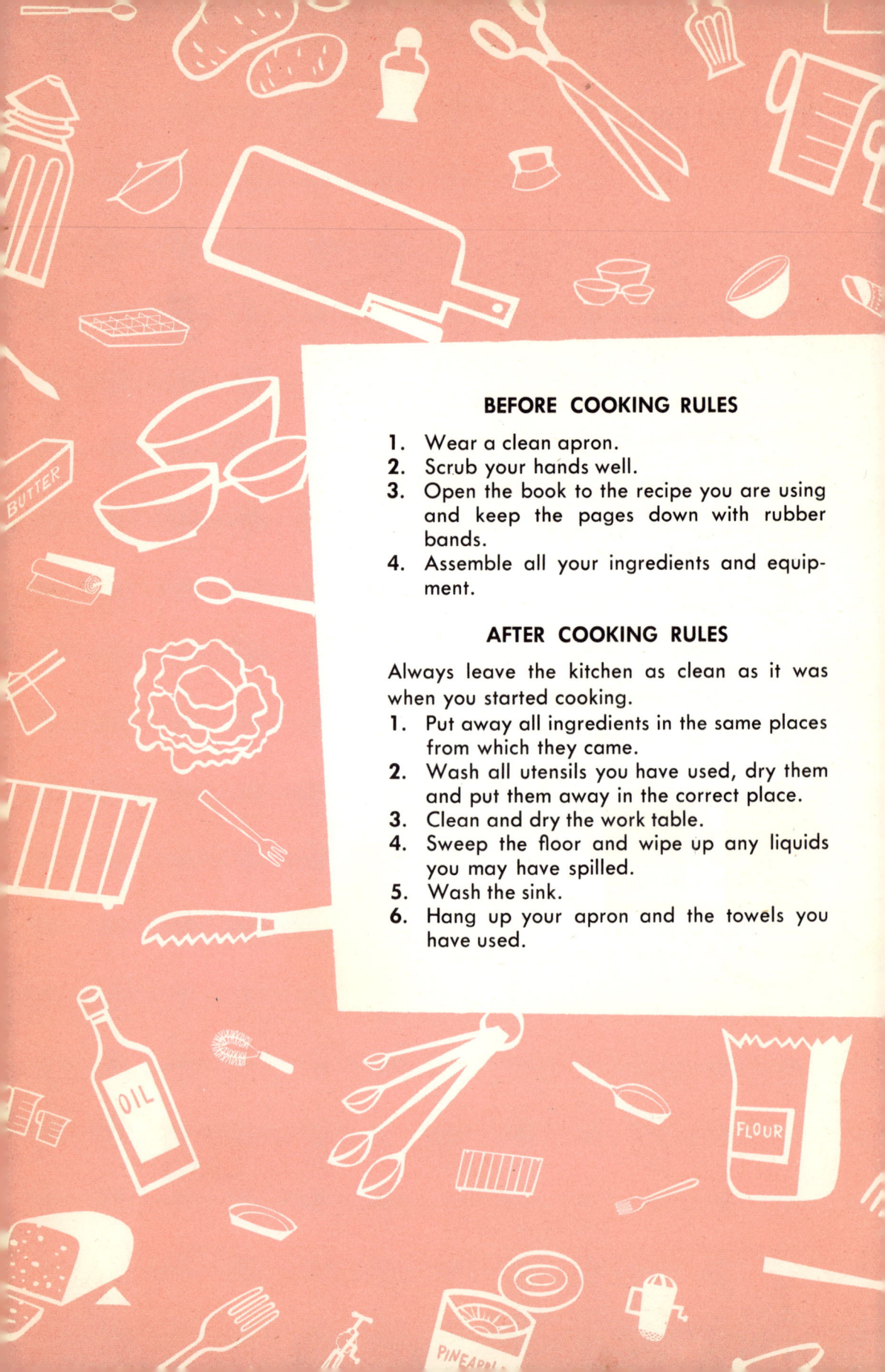

BEFORE COOKING RULES

1. Wear a clean apron.
2. Scrub your hands well.
3. Open the book to the recipe you are using and keep the pages down with rubber bands.
4. Assemble all your ingredients and equipment.

AFTER COOKING RULES

Always leave the kitchen as clean as it was when you started cooking.

1. Put away all ingredients in the same places from which they came.
2. Wash all utensils you have used, dry them and put them away in the correct place.
3. Clean and dry the work table.
4. Sweep the floor and wipe up any liquids you may have spilled.
5. Wash the sink.
6. Hang up your apron and the towels you have used.

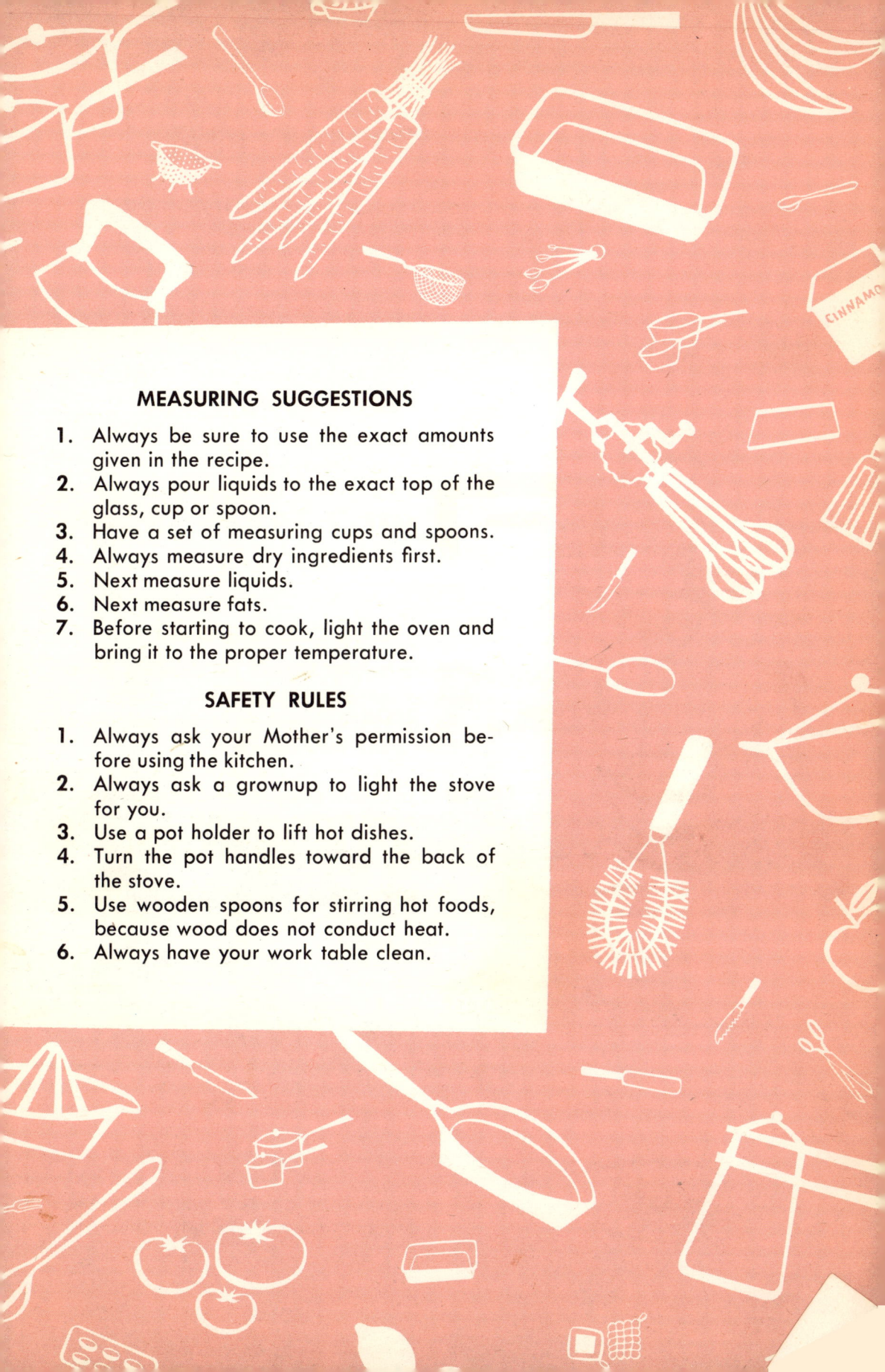

MEASURING SUGGESTIONS

1. Always be sure to use the exact amounts given in the recipe.
2. Always pour liquids to the exact top of the glass, cup or spoon.
3. Have a set of measuring cups and spoons.
4. Always measure dry ingredients first.
5. Next measure liquids.
6. Next measure fats.
7. Before starting to cook, light the oven and bring it to the proper temperature.

SAFETY RULES

1. Always ask your Mother's permission before using the kitchen.
2. Always ask a grownup to light the stove for you.
3. Use a pot holder to lift hot dishes.
4. Turn the pot handles toward the back of the stove.
5. Use wooden spoons for stirring hot foods, because wood does not conduct heat.
6. Always have your work table clean.

COOKING TERMS

BASTE — To pour liquid or fat over food which is cooking to moisten or flavor it.

DICE — To cut into tiny pieces.

BEAT — To mix by hand, by beater, or by electric mixer.

BAKE — To cook in an oven by dry heat.

BLEND — To mix shortening into dry ingredients.

BROIL — To cook under a direct fire.

CREAM — To mix shortening until smooth, soft and creamy.

FRY — To cook in hot fat or in deep oil.

ROAST — To cook, uncovered in the oven with moisture.

GRATE — To rub food on a grater.

BOIL — To cook in a liquid which has been brought to a boil and left there.

RULES OF ETIQUETTE

1. Always wash your hands before starting to eat.
2. Sit straight up on the chair, never slouch or lean.
3. Take only as much food as you know you can eat.
4. Eat quietly without making any undue noise.
5. Take only small bits of food and eat slowly.
6. Never reach across the table. Ask to have the food passed to you.
7. Don't be afraid to try a new food. All food is good.
8. Always say a prayer before and after eating.

> Thank you God,
>   For bread and meat,
> We pray that others too,
>   May have enough to eat.

HOW TO SET YOUR TABLE

PUT YOUR MILK OR WATER GLASS HERE

PUT YOUR NAPKIN HERE — FOLDED

SALAD

TEA

SOUP

HERE'S WHERE YOUR SILVERWARE GOES

AND HERE'S HOW YOUR TABLE SHOULD LOOK ALL READY TO SIT DOWN

Sabbath

IN every Jewish home, Friday is a busy day. Before sundown, the house is thoroughly cleaned and the Sabbath table set.

How nice the Sabbath table looks with it's beautiful white tablecloth, gleaming candlesticks, shiny silver wine cups and golden twisted challahs.

The Sabbath starts when Mother lights the candles. The children watch in fascination as she covers her eyes with her hands and in the glowing candlelight recites the blessing.

Soon afterwards, Father returns from the Friday night service. He pours the ruby red wine into his silver wine cup, raises it, and sings the Kiddush. Then, Father says the Ha-Motzi over the challah and gives a slice of it to everyone at the table.

Now, Mother serves the supper. Chicken soup, clear and golden, roast chicken, gefilte fish and scrumptious kugel. What a feast!

After supper, as soon as the dishes are cleared away, the family sings Shabbos songs.

The next morning everyone is up bright and early, and off to temple they go. The youngsters hold their own service. Some of them act as cantors; some of them read the Torah; and all of them join in singing the Sabbath prayers just as the grownups do.

The Sabbath ends when the first three stars appear in the sky. Then it is time for the Havdalah ceremony. Father recites the blessing over a cup of wine, a besomin box filled with spices and a twisted havdalah candle.

The Havdalah ceremony is really a way of saying "goodbye" to the Sabbath until next Friday night.

SHABBOS CANDLESTICK SALAD

INGREDIENTS

    canned sliced pineapple
    lettuce
    banana
    cherries

EQUIPMENT

    knife
    plate
    can opener

HOW TO MAKE

1. Wash a lettuce leaf and shake off the water.
2. Dry it on a plate.
3. Place a slice of pineapple on the lettuce leaf. This is the base for the candlestick.
4. Cut a banana half crosswise and stand it in the pineapple hole. This is the candle.
5. Place a cherry on top of the banana. This is the candle flame.

SABBATH DELIGHTS

No Sabbath table is complete without cookies. Here's an easy recipe that's a "delight" to taste.

INGREDIENTS

6 oz. package semi-sweet chocolate pieces
½ cup graham cracker crumbs
1 cup broken walnuts

EQUIPMENT

measuring cup
wax paper
wooden spoon
double boiler

HOW TO MAKE

1. Melt chocolate in a double boiler.
2. Stir in graham cracker crumbs and walnuts.
3. Drop mixture from teaspoon on to waxed paper.
4. Let stand until cool.
5. Make about fifteen delights.

FRIED FISH

Fish has always played an important part in all holiday and Sabbath meals. Serve cold fried fish at your Saturday and holiday afternoon meals. Serve fish with potato salad and pickles.

INGREDIENTS

one pound fish fillets
   haddock, halibut or flounder
teaspoon salt
pinch pepper
¼ cup matzoh meal
one tablespoon water
frying oil
one egg

EQUIPMENT

knife
fry pan
shallow plate
fork
paper toweling
bowl
measuring cup
egg beater

HOW TO MAKE

1. Beat one egg.
2. Add water to beaten egg and beat slightly.
3. Mix the pepper and salt with the matzoh meal.
4. Dip the fish slices in the beaten egg and then in the matzoh mixture.
5. Pour oil in fry pan until ⅛-inch deep.
6. Heat up the frying oil.
7. Carefully place the dipped fish slices in the hot oil.
8. Brown first one side and then the other.
9. Place fish on paper toweling and drain excess fat.
10. Serve hot or cold.

BOILED NOODLES

No Friday night meal is complete without Goldene Yuch, "golden" chicken soup. Noodles make a fine garnish for this Sabbath delicacy.

INGREDIENTS

¼ pound noodles
2 teaspoons salt
2 quarts boiling water

EQUIPMENT

large pot
colander

HOW TO MAKE

1. Break noodles into pieces about two inches long.
2. Add salt to boiling water.
3. Add noodles gradually.
4. Cook the noodles for about ten minutes, stirring constantly.
5. Drain in colander.
6. Rinse with boiling water.
7. Add noodles to soup.
8. Or, add 3 teaspoons melted butter and serve as a vegetable.

CANDIED SWEET POTATOES

Candied sweet potatoes will make a welcome addition to any Sabbath meal.

INGREDIENTS

4 sweet potatoes
½ cup brown sugar
¼ cup melted butter
¼ cup water

EQUIPMENT

large pot
scrubbing brush
saucepan
knife

HOW TO MAKE

1. Scrub the sweet potatoes well.
2. Cook the potatoes well for 35 minutes with their skins on.
3. Peel the jackets from the potatoes.
4. Slice each potato into quarters lengthwise.
5. Place sliced hot potatoes into saucepan.
6. Mix the sugar, butter and water together.
7. Add the mixture to the potatoes.
8. Simmer over low heat, turning frequently, till all the potatoes are glazed.

POTATO KUGEL

Kugel is one of those dishes that is everyone's favorite.

INGREDIENTS

5 potatoes
½ cup matzoh meal
3 eggs
salt and pepper
oil, shortening or butter

EQUIPMENT

grater
measuring cup
beater
baking dish or fry pan

HOW TO MAKE

1. Grate potatoes.
2. Add matzoh meal, salt and pepper.
3. Add well beaten egg yolks.
4. Beat egg whites stiff and fold into mixture.
5. Pour into greased baking dish.
6. Bake until brown on top.

Rosh Hashanah

THE first ten days of the Jewish New Year are called the High Holy Days. The High Holy Days start with the holiday of Rosh Hashanah which means New Year.

On Rosh Hashanah we go to temple and pray to God to send us His blessings in the coming year, and to thank Him for His blessings in the year which passed.

At the end of the service, it is customary for everyone to turn to his or her neighbor and wish him a "Happy New Year."

At home, Rosh Hashanah begins with the lighting of the candles and the singing of Kiddush.

On the table stands a round challah and a bowl of apple slices and honey. The round challah signifies a year without end. The apple slices and honey symbolizes our hope for a "sweet and happy New Year."

Yom Kippur

THE last day of the High Holy Days is called Yom Kippur, (Day of Atonement). This holiday is the holiest day of the year and is devoted to fasting and prayer.

The Yom Kippur eve service begins with the famous and beautiful Kol Nidre prayer; and the fasting is continuous for twenty-four hours.

On Yom Kippur eve, it is advisable to serve no spiced food. The meal at the end of the fast can be composed of regular Sabbath dishes.

HONEY CARROT TZIMMES

The Jewish word for carrots is "merin" which also means "to increase." During the High Holy Days carrots are served in various forms. They symbolize our hope for a year of "increasing" health and "increasing" prosperity.

INGREDIENTS

one pound carrots
¼ teaspoon salt
¼ cup honey
1 tablespoon flour
dash of lemon juice
3 tablespoons butter

EQUIPMENT

deep pot
knife
peeler
fry pan
measuring cup
measuring spoon

HOW TO MAKE

1. Peel carrots and cut into thin slices.
2. Cover carrots with cold water and cook for ten minutes.
3. Add the salt, honey and lemon juice.
4. Let boil gently for about fifteen minutes; until liquid has been reduced to about half.
5. Brown flour in hot melted butter.
6. Add to carrot mixture and shake gently.
7. Cook for five minutes more.

ROSH HASHANAH CLUSTERS

Start the New Year right. Here's a "treat," that will make the New Year "sweet."

INGREDIENTS

1 cup semi-sweet chocolate bits
8 marshmallows cut into small pieces
¼ cup seedless raisins
¾ cup chopped walnuts

EQUIPMENT

double boiler
measuring cup
teaspoon
wax paper
wooden spoon

HOW TO MAKE

1. Melt chocolate over double boiler.
2. Mix in marshmallows, raisins, and walnuts.
3. Stir till all ingredients are coated.
4. Drop by teaspoon on wax paper.
5. Let stand and cool.
6. Makes about 18 clusters.

STUFFED EGGS

To the Jews the egg has always been a symbol of life. It is appropriate to serve egg dishes during the High Holy Days in the hope that the coming new year will be filled with life and happiness.

INGREDIENTS

3 hardboiled eggs
2 tablespoons mayonnaise
¼ teaspoon salt
speck pepper
1 teaspoon diced onion
⅛ teaspoon mustard

EQUIPMENT

knife
fork
wax paper
measuring spoon

HOW TO MAKE

1. Shell the eggs, cut in half lengthwise and lay whites aside.
2. Carefully remove yolks and mash.
3. Mix the yolks with the salt, mayonnaise, pepper, mustard and diced onion.
4. Refill the egg whites.

HONEY COOKIES

Honey is symbolic of the wish for a "sweet and happy New Year." Serve these cookies and start the New Year right.

INGREDIENTS

1 cup butter
½ cup sugar
4 tablespoons honey
2½ cups sifted all purpose flour

EQUIPMENT

spoon
wax paper
rolling pin
cookie cutters
baking sheet
measuring cup
measuring spoon
fork

HOW TO MAKE

1. Cream butter, sugar and honey.
2. Add flour slowly.
3. Mix thoroughly to a smooth dough.
4. Chill in refrigerator for two hours.
5. Roll out on wax paper to about ½ inch thick.
6. Shape with a cookie cutter.
7. Place on ungreased cookie sheet.
8. Bake in oven at 300 degrees for 25 minutes.

BAKED POTATO

A baked potato is a welcome addition to any meal.

INGREDIENTS
potatoes
salt

EQUIPMENT
oven rack

HOW TO MAKE
1. Preheat oven to 400 degrees.
2. Wash the potatoes well.
3. Sprinkle well with salt.
4. Bake on rack for one hour.

Sukkos

SUKKOS (Feast of Booths) is celebrated for eight days. On this occasion we recall the booths in which the Hebrews lived during their wanderings from Egypt to the Promised Land.

On this holiday, we too build booths and roof them with boughs and vines of green, just as our ancestors did thousands of years ago.

Sukkos is also known as the Harvest Festival. In honor of the festival we decorate the inside of the Sukkoh with fruits and flowers.

As symbols of the ancient harvest in the land of Israel, we recite blessings over the Lulov (palm) and the Esrog (citron).

Since Sukkos is a Harvest Festival, it is customary to eat fruits, vegetables and dairy dishes.

Simchas Torah

THE last day of Sukkos is known as Simchas Torah, (Rejoicing of the Law). On this day we read the last chapter of the Torah and we start our Torah all over again by also reading the first chapter.

After the reading, all the Torahs are taken from the Ark and the Hakofos (procession) begins. The holy scrolls are carried around the temple seven times. Even those who are not carrying Torahs, join in the parade. They march behind the Torahs carrying flags and singing happy Simchas Torah songs. Before the Hakofos, the children are given bags of candy and nuts and a juicy red apple.

With Simchas Torah, the holiday of Sukkos comes to a happy end.

SIMCHAS TORAH FLAG SALAD

INGREDIENTS
- canned peaches
- lettuce

EQUIPMENT
- knife
- plate
- toothpicks
- paper
- can opener
- scissors

HOW TO MAKE

1. Wash a lettuce leaf, shake off the water and lay it on the plate.
2. Place half a peach, flat side up.
3. Cut out a piece of paper into a flag, and put it on a toothpick.
4. Stick the toothpick into the peach.
5. You can color the flag or write the name of the guest on the flag.

PENUCHE

INGREDIENTS

2 cups brown sugar
⅔ cup milk
4 tablespoons butter
1 cup nuts or raisins
½ teaspoon vanilla
butter, oil or shortening

EQUIPMENT

measuring cup
measuring spoon
wooden spoon
saucepan
beater

HOW TO MAKE

1. Mix sugar, milk and butter in saucepan.
2. Bring to boil.
3. Cook slowly for fifteen minutes.
4. Remove from fire.
5. Add nuts and vanilla and beat till creamy.
6. Pour into shallow greased pan to cool.
7. When cool, cut into squares.

CARROT RAISIN SALAD

Serve this salad at your Sukkos Party.

INGREDIENTS

2 carrots
½ cup raisins
mayonnaise
lettuce

EQUIPMENT

scrubbing brush
cutting board
knife
bowl
measuring cup
spoon

HOW TO MAKE

1. Wash a lettuce leaf and shake off the water.
2. Lay it on a plate.
3. Wash the carrots and dice.
4. Dice the raisins.
5. Place raisins and carrots in bowl.
6. Mix in mayonnaise.
7. Place a scoop of salad on a lettuce leaf.
8. Make 4 portions.

BAKED BANANAS

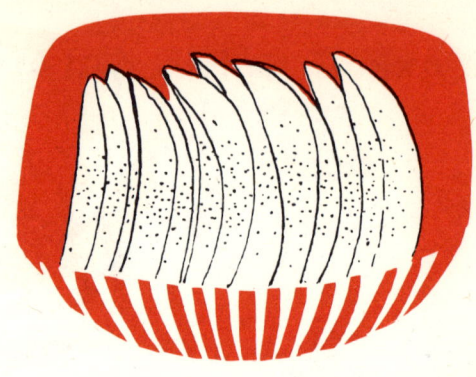

Fruit dishes and fruit desserts are traditional for Sukkos. Try this simple recipe on your family. They'll want you to make it often.

INGREDIENTS
- 6 hard bananas
- 2 tablespoons butter
- 2 tablespoons brown sugar

EQUIPMENT
- baking pan

HOW TO MAKE
1. Peel green firm bananas and place in greased baking pan.
2. Brush with butter.
3. Sprinkle with brown sugar.
4. Bake at 375 degrees for 18 minutes.
5. Serve as a hot vegetable.
6. Or, as a dessert with cream.

MEATBURGERS

Meatburgers are everyone's favorite. Try these as a main dish for one of your Sukkos meals.

INGREDIENTS

1 pound ground meat
¼ cup bread crumbs
1 egg
1 teaspoon salt
½ teaspoon pepper
½ cup canned tomatoes

EQUIPMENT

fork
baking pan
knife
measuring cup
measuring spoon

HOW TO MAKE

1. Dice canned tomatoes.
2. Mix ground meat with bread crumbs, egg, salt, pepper and diced canned tomatoes.
3. Shape into patties one inch thick.
4. Bake in hot oven at 450 degrees for twelve minutes.

The Story Of Chanukah

MANY years ago, a wicked Syrian king, named Antiochus, captured the land of Palestine. He ordered the Jews to give up their religion and worship his idols. All who refused to obey the king's command, were put to death.

Under the leadership of Mattathias and his five sons, the Jews rebelled. Even though they were greatly outnumbered by the Syrian forces, the courageous Maccabean army defeated the enemy and captured Jerusalem.

Immediately, they marched out to the Holy Temple and smashed the idols that the Syrians had put there. When they had cleaned and repaired the temple, everyone gathered to celebrate the "rededication."

The High Priest could find only one flask of Holy Oil with which to light the new Menorah. This was just enough oil to burn for one day. But a great miracle happened! Much to everyone's amazement, this little flask of oil burned for eight days and nights. Because of this miracle we celebrate Chanukah for eight days.

Chanukah comes on the 25th day of Kislev, in the deep of the winter. On the first night of Chanukah we light one candle and every night thereafter we light an additional one until our menorah has eight candles standing in a row.

When the menorah is lit and the blessings are sung, the festivities begin. Everyone gathers around the menorah and joins in playing draydel games and exchanging Chanukah gifts.

The traditional food for Chanukah is "latkes," (potato pancakes). The reason for eating this food is uncertain.

Some say we eat latkes because the Maccabees used to eat them. When chasing their enemies, they did not have time to stop and eat a regular meal so they ate latkes which are easy and quick to prepare.

CHANUKAH COOKIES

If you do not have any cookie cutters, here are some patterns for you to trace. Make them of cardboard and cut around them.

INGREDIENTS

2 cups flour
1 cup sugar
½ teaspoon salt
2 teaspoons baking powder
1 egg
⅓ cup butter
¼ cup milk
1 teaspoon vanilla
butter, oil or shortening

EQUIPMENT

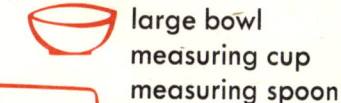

large bowl
measuring cup
measuring spoon
beater
sifter
bread board
rolling pin
cookie cutters
cookie sheet

HOW TO MAKE

1. Cream butter and sugar in a large bowl.
2. In another bowl, beat the egg and add the milk and flavoring.
3. Stir both mixtures into a large bowl.
4. Sift together the flour, salt, and baking powder.
5. Add these ingredients into the large mixture and stir well.
6. Place the dough into the refrigerator for one hour.
7. Dust a bread board and rolling pin with flour.
8. Roll out the cool dough about ¼ of an inch thick.
9. Cut into fancy shapes with cookie cutters.
10. Place on greased cookie sheet.
11. Bake in oven for 12 minutes.

CHANUKAH LATKES

Latkes, latkes, yum, yum, yum,
Try this recipe and you'll make some.
Latkes, latkes, they'll taste fine,
I'll bet you'll make them all the time.

INGREDIENTS

2 large potatoes
½ an onion
1 egg
¼ cup flour
1 teaspoon salt
oil, butter or shortening

EQUIPMENT

grater
mixing bowl
beater
fry pan
spoon
paper toweling
spatula
measuring cup
paring knife

HOW TO MAKE

1. Peel the potatoes and grate.
2. Peel and grate the onion.
3. Add the flour, salt, and egg.
4. Mix thoroughly till smooth.
5. Grease the fry pan.
6. Drop the batter into the hot fry pan, making each pancake about three inches in diameter.
7. Fry till brown on one side; then turn to other side and also fry till brown.
8. Lift from fry pan and place on paper toweling till fat drains off.

MARSHMALLOW POPS

The marshmallow pops will really make a hit at your Chanukah party.

INGREDIENTS
- marshmallows
- water
- chopped pecans

EQUIPMENT
- saucepan
- wax paper
- short drinking straws
- long fork

HOW TO MAKE
1. Stick marshmallow on to long kitchen fork.
2. Steam over boiling water until sticky.
3. Drop marshmallow on chopped pecan and roll around until coated.
4. Place on wax paper till coated marshmallow is firm.
5. Stick short drinking straw into each.

DRAYDEL SALAD

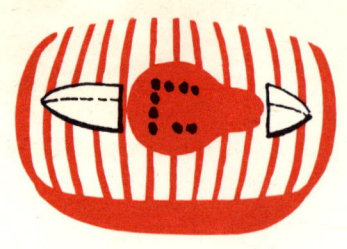

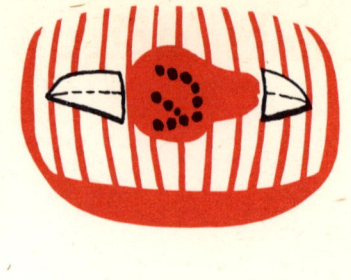

Here is an easy Chanukah surprise to make.

INGREDIENTS
    canned pear halves
    raisins
    banana

EQUIPMENT
    knife
    can opener

HOW TO MAKE
1. Place one-half pear on plate, flat side down.
2. Use raisins to make a draydel letter.
3. Cut banana into long slices.
4. Use one slice for the handle of the draydel.
5. Use a short slice for the tip of the draydel.

PANCAKES

INGREDIENTS

one cup pancake mix
one cup milk
shortening, oil or butter
maple syrup

EQUIPMENT

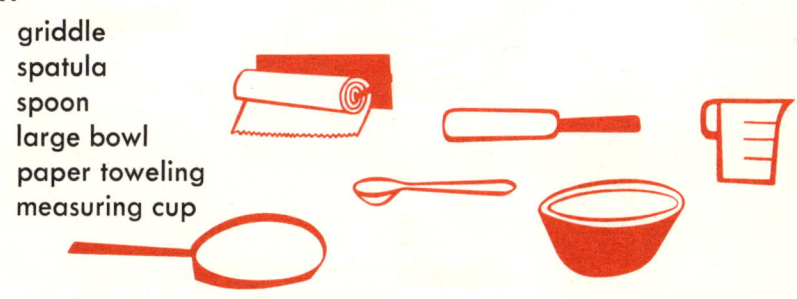

griddle
spatula
spoon
large bowl
paper toweling
measuring cup

HOW TO MAKE

1. To one cup of milk add one cup of pancake mix.
2. Stir well and leave no lumps.
3. Heat the griddle and grease with shortening; keep the heat on medium.
4. Spoon pancake mixture on to hot griddle; each pancake should be about four inches in diameter.
5. When edges look brown and the bubbles start to break, turn the pancake with your spatula.
6. Cook till brown on the other side.
7. Remove from skillet and serve with butter and syrup.

Chamishah Osor B'Shevat

ARBOR DAY in Israel is called Chamishah Osor B'Shevat (which means the fifteenth day of the month of Shevat). It is a very big and important holiday there.

On this day, all the the synagogues are closed and the children are taken on picnics. While picnicing the children play games and plant trees. What fun tree planting is!

Everyone helps. Some dig holes, some pour water, others help guide the saplings into the moist holes. When the trees are in place, everyone helps pack the rich soil around the tiny tree roots.

Israeli children know that trees are very important and serve many useful purposes.

Some trees drain swamps to make Israel a healthier place in which to live. Others can be made into lumber with which to build new homes, schools, ships, etc. Other trees help hold the soil in place so that wind and flood cannot carry it away.

Some trees bear fruit and give shade from the hot Israeli sun.

On Chamishah Osor B'Shevat, we too go on picnics and parties and enjoy the fruits of Israel.

We eat oranges, dates, figs and grapes, bokser (Saint John's bread), and cookies in the shape of trees.

STUFFED DATES

You won't need a stove to make this.

INGREDIENTS
dates
nuts
sugar

EQUIPMENT
knife
wax paper

HOW TO MAKE
1. Remove pits from the dates.
2. Put half a walnut or pecan in the cavity.
3. Close up the date.
4. Roll the dates in sugar; plain or powdered.

STUFFED PRUNES

INGREDIENTS
- prunes
- marshmallow
- peanut butter
- sugar

EQUIPMENT
- double boiler
- knife
- wax paper

HOW TO MAKE
1. Steam some prunes in a double boiler for ten minutes.
2. Cool them and remove the stones.
3. Stuff them with marshmallows or peanut butter.
4. Roll them in sugar on the wax paper.

Purim

MANY years ago, in the far away land of Persia, there lived a King named Ahasueras. One day the King decided that he needed a new queen, so he sent his messengers to look for the most beautiful maiden in the whole land of Persia.

They found a beautiful young Jewish girl named Esther, who was living with her Uncle Mordecai. When the King saw lovely Esther, he fell in love with her immediately and chose her for his new queen.

At that time, the King's chief minister was a wicked man named Haman. He wanted everyone to bow down to him and almost everyone did. But Mordecai refused. Haman became very angry at Mordecai and at all the Jews. He decided to have all the Jews in the land of Persia killed. Lots were cast, and the thirteenth day of Adar was the date chosen for the terrible deed. Of course the Jews were frightened, Mordecai begged Esther to save her people.

Soon the King noticed that the Queen was unhappy. When he asked Esther what was worrying her, she replied, "Oh King, Haman is going to kill my people on the thirteenth day of Adar. He has built gallows on which to hang my Uncle Mordecai. Please save my people and my Uncle."

Ahasueras did not want beautiful Esther to be unhappy. The King called his palace guards and ordered them to hang Haman on the very gallows he had prepared for Mordecai.

So on the thirteenth day of Adar, the Jews, instead of being killed, celebrated a happy holiday. They called the day Purim, which means "lots."

Today, the holiday of Purim starts with the reading of the Megillah in the temple. Everytime Haman's name is mentioned, the children stamp their feet, rattle their graggers, and make lots of noise.

After the reading of the Megillah, the fun really starts. In Israel, they stage outdoor carnivals and parades. In our homes, we celebrate by making a special Purim feast called a Seudah, and by sending Shalach Monos to our friends and relatives.

The traditional food for Purim is Hamantaschen, a three cornered cake filled with poppy or plum filling. Some say we eat Hamantaschen because Haman wore a three cornered hat; some even say that Haman's ears were three cornered just like a donkey's ears.

HAMANTASCHEN

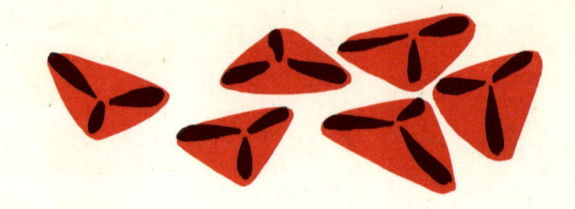

Follow the recipe for Chanukah cookies on page 35.

1. Roll the dough out thin.
2. Cut into rounds of two and a half inches.
3. Place spoonful of hamanteschen filling in the center of each round.
4. Draw up three sides and pinch the sides together in the shape of a triangle.
5. Place on buttered cookie sheet.
6. Bake at 375 degrees for 40 minutes.

HAMANTASCHEN PRUNE FILLING

INGREDIENTS

grated lemon rind
2 tablespoons lemon juice
½ pound prunes

EQUIPMENT

pot
colander
knife
cutting board
grater

HOW TO MAKE

1. Soak prunes in water for twelve hours.
2. Cook in water till soft.
3. Drain well.
4. Remove stone from prunes.
5. Dice the prunes.
6. Mix diced prunes with lemon rind and lemon juice.

PARTY LEMONADE

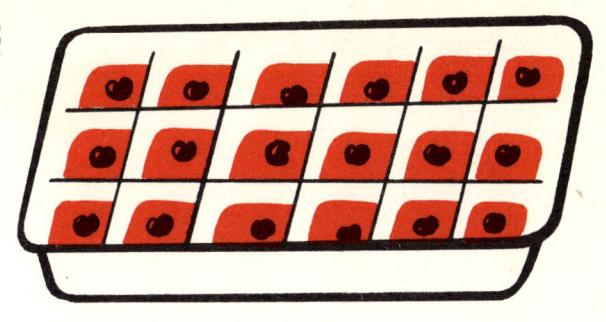

Are you making a Purim party? Serve this special lemonade and listen to the "oohs" and "ahs."

INGREDIENTS
frozen lemonade
maraschino cherries

EQUIPMENT
ice tray

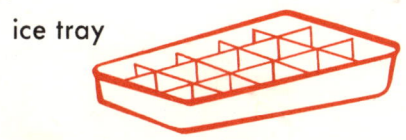

HOW TO MAKE
1. Place one cherry in each cube.
2. Fill ice tray with water.
3. Place in freezer.
4. Mix lemonade as per instructions on can.
5. Put a frozen cube in each glass of lemonade.

PURIM HAT COOKIES

The Jews in ancient Persia wore hats that looked something like these cookies.

INGREDIENTS

one cup flour
shortening
marshmallows
½ cup quick oats
¼ cup butter
¼ cup brown sugar
¼ cup white sugar
½ tablespoon vanilla
1 egg
½ tablespoon salt

EQUIPMENT

big bowl
sifter
wooden spoon
paper towels
wax paper
cookie sheets
egg beater
measuring cup
measuring spoon

HOW TO MAKE

1. Preheat oven to 375 degrees.
2. Put ¼ cup of butter in large bowl and beat till smooth.
3. Slowly add ¼ cup brown sugar and ¼ cup white sugar; beat till fluffy.
4. Beat in ½ tablespoon of vanilla and ½ tablespoon of salt.
5. Add egg and stir till completely mixed.
6. To mixture add ½ cup oats.
7. Sift flour onto wax paper.
8. Add one cup of sifted flour to mixture and mix well.
9. Grease the cookie sheets.
10. Put spoonfulls of mixture on the cookie sheet; one spoonful to a cookie and flatten each one.
11. Bake for eight minutes at 375 degrees.
12. Remove from stove and place a marshmallow on each cookie and serve.

QUEEN ESTHER SALAD

INGREDIENTS
pineapple
almonds
cottage cheese
raisins

EQUIPMENT
knife
plate
can opener

HOW TO MAKE
1. Form a ball of cottage cheese and place in center of plate.
2. Place raisins in ball of cheese to make features of a face.
3. Cut a pineapple slice in half.
4. Crown the face with the half slice of pineapple.
5. Decorate Queen Esther's crown with almond halves.

NOAH'S ARK COOKIES

Cookies are favorites for Sholach Monos baskets. Make these animal cookies for your baskets.

INGREDIENTS

    1 package semi-sweet chocolate pieces
    ⅓ cup white corn syrup
    2 ounces rice cereal

EQUIPMENT

    double boiler
    measuring cup
    jelly roll pan
    animal cutters

HOW TO MAKE

1. Melt chocolate in double boiler.
2. Stir in corn syrup.
3. Pour in rice cereal.
4. Mix until all kernels are coated.
5. Spread in jelly roll pan.
6. Cut with animal cutter.

Passover

PASSOVER is also known as the Festival of Freedom. On this holiday, at the Seder, we relive and retell the story of the Exodus.

We tell the story of the Israelites who were slaves to the Pharaoh in the land of Egypt more than 3000 years ago. Under the leadership of Moses, the Hebrews were at last set free.

They left in such great haste, they did not have time to leaven their bread.

When Moses and his followers reached the Red Sea, they received word that Pharaoh had changed his mind. He and his army were racing to recapture the Hebrews. Moses prayed to God. He then lifted his staff, and a miracle happened. The waters of the Red Sea parted, leaving a wide path through which Moses led his people to the other side. Behind them came the Egyptian army with its many chariots and horsemen. As Pharaoh's men were crossing the deep sea, Moses again lifted his staff. This time the water swiftly returned, and the entire Egyptian army was drowned.

Springtime is Pesach time. Everyone is busy preparing for the festive holiday.

At last the long awaited Seder night arrives. The table is set with a Passover plate with the five special passover symbols. Bitter herbs for the bitterness of slavery in the land of Egypt; A bone for the paschal lamb; Harosseth, which looks like the clay the Jews made into bricks; Green herbs, which stands for the springtime; An egg, which is a symbol of life.

Father arranges three matzohs in the beautiful embroidered matzoh cover and then sits down on his Pesach throne. Everyone opens his Hagadah. The Seder has begun.

Father stands, and raising his wine cup, sings the Kiddush. Then the youngest child proudly asks the Four Questions and everyone reads the story of Passover.

During the meal, the Afikomen which Father has hidden, disappears. It must be found before the Seder can be continued. Soon Father opens the door to admit the Prophet Elijah, who visits each Jewish home on Seder night. At the end of the Seder everyone joins in singing the Passover songs.

Passover is the holiday most closely associated with food. During this holiday we omit all leaven from our meals. Dried beans, grains, breads, baking soda and yeasts are forbidden. Instead of flour, we use matzoh products: Matzoh meal, matzoh flour, matzoh cereal.

Passover is a busy time for Mother, with all the cooking and baking and cleaning, Mother will appreciate all the help she can get.

Let's help by setting the Passover table. First we'll cover the table with a white tablecloth, and set out the plates and silverware. Alongside each setting, place a wine cup and in the center of the table the special cup for Elijah the Prophet.

Now arrange the Seder place with all the Passover symbols. Follow the picture and place each symbol in its correct position.

On the following page you will find the recipe for charoses.

Underneath the seder plate place the matzoh cover with a matzoh in each of its three compartments. Don't forget to place a Haggadah at each setting so that everyone can participate in the Seder.

CHAROSES

INGREDIENTS
- one apple
- ½ cup finely chopped nuts
- ½ tablespoon cinnamon
- 1 tablespoon sugar
- ½ tablespoon wine

EQUIPMENT
- grater
- fork
- paring knife
- measuring cup
- measuring spoon

HOW TO MAKE
1. Peel apple and grate.
2. Chop nuts very fine.
3. Mix the grated apple, chopped nuts, cinnamon, sugar and wine together.
4. Blend thoroughly until free of lumps.

MATZOH BRIE

INGREDIENTS

2 matzohs
boiling water
2 eggs
pepper
salt
honey
butter, shortening, oil, or fat

EQUIPMENT

colander
beater
large fry pan

HOW TO MAKE

1. Break two matzohs into medium sized pieces, and place in colander.
2. Pour hot water over them and drain quickly.
3. Beat eggs well.
4. Add beaten eggs to matzohs.
5. Add salt and pepper to taste.
6. Heat a large fry pan and grease.
7. Add matzoh and egg mixture to hot fry pan.
8. Cook over low heat till brown on one side.
9. Turn gently and cook other side till brown.
10. Serve hot.
11. Pour honey over matzoh brie.

PASSOVER KUGEL

INGREDIENTS

3 matzos
one egg yolk
one apple
butter or shortening
salt
pepper

EQUIPMENT

large dish
beater
paring knife
chopping board
wax paper
casserole dish

HOW TO MAKE

1. Soak matzos in water for two minutes.
2. Squeeze out as much water as possible.
3. Peel and dice the apple.
4. Add one tablespoon of butter or shortening and the diced apple to the matzos.
5. Beat yolk into the mixture and season with salt and pepper.
6. Beat egg white until stiff.
7. Add the beaten egg white; handle egg white gently.
8. Pour into greased casserole dish.
9. Bake in slow oven for one hour or until top has a nice brown crust.

PASSOVER MACAROONS

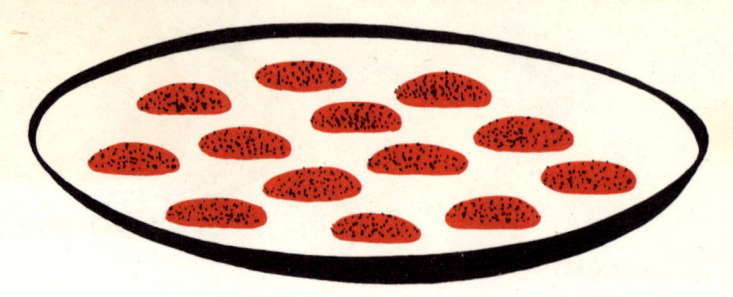

INGREDIENTS
one four ounce package shredded coconut
2 egg whites
½ cup powdered sugar
½ teaspoon lemon juice
butter, oil or shortening

EQUIPMENT
glass bowl
measuring cup
cookie sheet
egg beater

HOW TO MAKE
1. Put whites into a bowl and beat till stiff.
2. Add sugar to stiff egg whites; blend.
3. Add the lemon and continue beating until light and smooth.
4. Add the shredded coconut; mix thoroughly.
5. Drop spoonfuls on to a greased cookie sheet.
6. Bake in an oven at 275 degrees for 40 minutes.

PEANUT BRITTLE

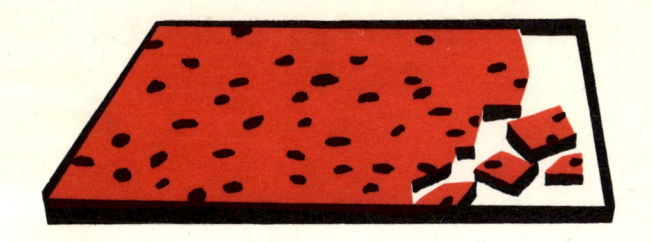

You can substitute any kind of nuts you wish. Everybody likes peanut brittle. Make it for Passover.

INGREDIENTS
    1 cup sugar
    1 cup shelled peanuts
        butter, oil or shortening

EQUIPMENT
    heavy iron frying pan
    wooden spoon
    oblong pan
    measuring cup

HOW TO MAKE
1. Melt sugar in the frying pan over a low fire.
2. Stir the sugar with your wooden spoon as it melts.
3. When it is light brown, stir in the nuts.
4. Pour the mixture into a greased pan.
5. When it has cooled break the candy into pieces.

CANDIED APPLE WEDGES

Candied fruit slices are great favorites for Passover. Try these apple wedges on your family.

INGREDIENTS

3 cups granulated sugar
1 1/8 cups water
1/2 teaspoon salt
3 pared apples

EQUIPMENT

large saucepan
measuring cup
wire drain rack
wax paper
apple corer

HOW TO MAKE

1. In large saucepan place 2 1/2 cups granulated sugar, salt and water.
2. Heat and stir till sugar dissolves.
3. Boil for ten minutes till you get a rich syrup.
4. Cut pared apples into eighths lengthwise; trim and core.
5. Lay pieces into syrup and boil gently until most of syrup is absorbed.
6. Drain on rack in shallow pan.
7. Roll pieces in remaining half cup of sugar.
8. After apples dry for several hours, roll in sugar once more.

Lag B'Omer

LAG B'OMER is a gay, spring holiday. We celebrate it by picnicing, going on hikes and playing with bows and arrows. The holiday commemorates the day the plague among Rabbi Akiba's students stopped.

Akiba was a fearless Rabbi who lived in a sad and troubled period of Jewish history. The Romans had conquered Palestine, captured Jerusalem and destroyed the Temple. Many Jews were killed and the study of Torah was forbidden.

Akiba hid in the forest and continued to study and teach the Torah. His students disguised themselves as hunters by carrying bows and arrows. Should the Roman soldiers find them, this was their excuse for being in the forest.

One time a plague struck Rabbi Akiba's students and killed many of them. Suddenly on Lag B'omer the plague stopped and the study of Torah was continued again.

Lag B'omer means the thirty-third day of counting the Omer. This holiday is also known as the Scholars Holiday in honor of Rabbi Akiba and his fearless students.

One of the most famous of Rabbi Akiba's student was Bar Kochba. He was a very brave, fearless, and strong warrior. Under his leadership the Jews fought the Romans for more than three years. Bar Kochba and his men recaptured Jerusalem, and started to rebuild the Temple that the Romans had destroyed.

But the Romans returned with more and more soldiers. The Jews retreated to the fortress city of Bethar. On the ninth day of Av, (Tisha B'av) the Romans capture the city and killed Bar Kochba.

There are no traditional foods for Lag B'omer. Instead we go on pack picnic lunches and eat out of doors just like Rabbi Akiba and his students did thousands of years ago.

Lag B'Omer is the time we all go on picnics. Picnics mean sandwiches. Here are a few hints on sandwich-making which can make your picnic lunch a success.

HINTS FOR SANDWICH MAKING

1. Make your sandwiches from a variety of breads and rolls.
2. Cream butter before spreading.
3. Avoid making sandwiches with moist fillings in advance, since the bread becomes soggy.
4. Wrap each sandwich in wax paper.
5. Use a variety of fillings.
6. Vegetables, such as tomatoes, lettuce and cucumbers should be prepared and added just before serving.

SANDWICH FILLINGS

1. Cream cheese and lox.
2. Cream cheese and jelly.
3. Sliced egg and tomato.
4. Egg and diced celery.
5. Tuna, celery and mayonnaise.
6. Sardines and egg.
7. Chopped salmon and onions.
8. Peanut butter and jelly.
9. Swiss cheese and mustard.

LAG B'OMER BULL'S-EYE

Rabbi Akiba's scholars used to disguise themselves as hunters. With their bows and arrows they used to shoot at targets such as this egg bull's-eye.
Try this recipe. I'll bet it hits the target.

INGREDIENTS
white bread
butter
egg
salt

EQUIPMENT
fry pan
small glass

HOW TO MAKE
1. Use a glass and cut a hole in a slice of white bread.
2. Grease the fry pan with butter.
3. Place bread with hole in pan and toast till bottom side is brown.
4. Turn bread over, brown side up.
5. Crack the egg, and drop the egg into the hole.
6. Fry until egg is done.

CHOCOLATE PEPPERMINTS

Try these peppermints on your Lag B'Omer picnic.

INGREDIENTS

4 squares bitter chocolate
1/8 cup sweetened condensed milk
1/8 cup honey
1/8 teaspoon salt
few drops peppermint extract

EQUIPMENT

double boiler
wooden mixing spoon
measuring cup
measuring spoon
waxed paper

HOW TO MAKE

1. Melt chocolate in a double boiler.
2. Stir in condensed milk, honey, salt, and peppermint.
3. Allow to cool and drop chocolate from a teaspoon on wax paper.
4. Makes about two dozen chocolate pieces.

Shevuoth

SHEVUOTH (Festival of Weeks) is celebrated seven weeks after the Passover Holidays. It marks the birthday of the Ten Commandments which Moses received on Mount Sinai. At that time, Moses, at God's command, gathered the Israelites at the foot of the Mount. They waited and they waited. On the third day, a thick cloud settled on the mountain. The earth shook. Everyone trembled. Amid thunder and lightning, they heard the voice of God calling out the Ten Commandments.

Shevuoth also celebrates the Harvest Festival. At this season the Jewish farmers journeyed to the Temple with the first fruits of their fields. These gifts were collected by the priests and were distributed to the poor people of the land. Shevuoth is also known as Hag Habikurim which means "first ripe fruits."

Today, we celebrate Shevuoth by attending Synagogue, where we read the Ten Commandments and a special hymn called Akdomus. This prayer describes the wisdom of the Torah and the coming of the Messiah.

It is also customary to read the Book of Ruth, which describes the harvest in ancient Palestine and tells how the poor people of the land were allowed to pick up the fallen ears of grain during the harvest.

To remind us of the Harvest Festival, homes and synagogues are decorated with green leaves, flowers and fruit.

Religious schools hold their Confirmation and Graduation exercises during this season.

Because the Torah has been compared to "milk and honey," sweet dairy dishes are usually served on Shevuoth. Blintzes (cheese filled pancakes) is a favorite dish.

CRACKER CHEESE BLINTZES

INGREDIENTS

10 soda crackers
4 eggs
salt
½ pound dry cottage cheese
2 tablespoons sugar
cinnamon
butter, oil or shortening

EQUIPMENT

2 mixing bowls
beater
griddle

HOW TO MAKE

1. Beat two eggs well.
2. Add ¼ cup of milk and pinch of salt to the beaten eggs.

TO MAKE FILLING

1. Combine cottage cheese, two eggs, two tablespoons of sugar and pinch of cinnamon.
2. Mix well.
3. Place a quantity of filling between two crackers.
4. Dip cracker and cheese sandwich in egg and milk mixture.
5. Place sandwich on hot greased griddle.
6. Fry on both sides till brown.

TOMATO FLOWER SALAD

Shevuoth is a time for serving "harvest fruits." Vegetables, fruits, and dairy dishes are traditional delights.

INGREDIENTS
- tomatoes
- paprika
- cottage cheese
- french dressing
- lettuce

EQUIPMENT
- knife

HOW TO MAKE
1. Cut away core of tomato.
2. Cut the tomato into wedges. Do not cut wedges all the way through.
3. Place wedged tomato on washed lettuce leaf.
4. Fill tomato with cottage cheese.
5. Sprinkle with paprika and french dressing.

QUICK TRUFFLES

The Torah is said to be "nutritious as honey, and as good as milk." Try these "nutritious" truffles with a glass of "milk."

INGREDIENTS

1 package semi-sweet chocolate bits
3/8 cup sweetened condensed milk
1/2 cup chopped walnuts
1/2 teaspoon vanilla extract
few grains of salt

EQUIPMENT

double boiler
measuring cup
measuring spoon
wax paper
shallow pan
wooden spoon

HOW TO MAKE

1. Melt chocolate in double boiler.
2. Stir in condensed milk, walnuts, vanilla and salt.
3. Pour into wax lined pan.
4. Cool for a few hours.
5. When firm, cut into squares.